SPILLED BEER
WET PAPER

Selected Poems by Bill Butler

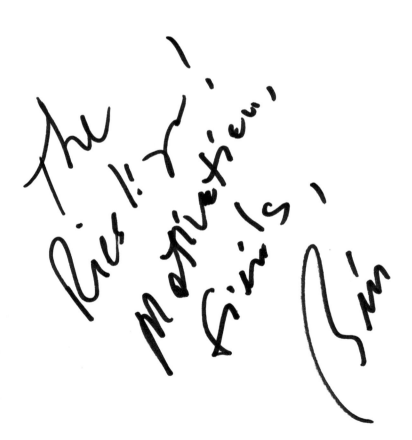

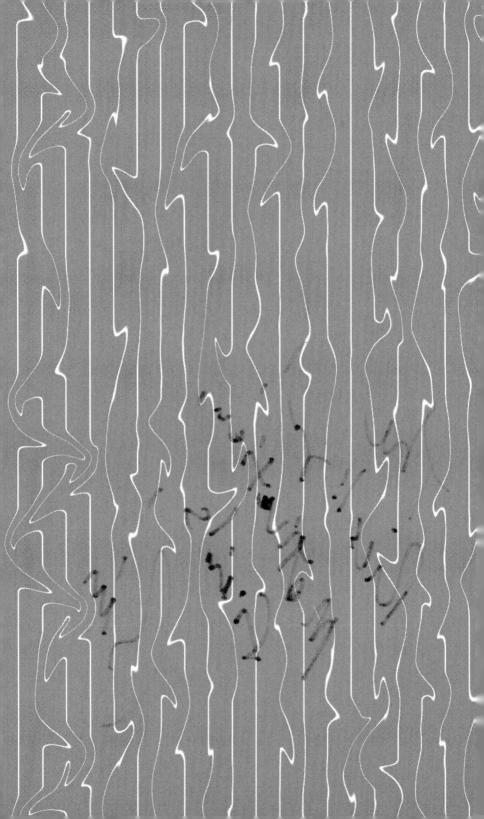

A HISTORY OF RAVENS

The ravens are not quiet.
They gather,
  slowly,
  an unkindness.
The ravens in the pines,
  debating formally,
  discussing at length our weaknesses, foibles.
Leaning conspiratorially forward,
  judging us,
  full disclosure,
  we are noted as unremarkable.
In this history of ravens
  swinging on fragrant pine limbs,
  the wind sighing through the needles,
  I hear their comments.
 Leaning forward,
  judged lacking in most things important,
  Glittering yellow eyes, following me,
  I am measured,
We are measured.

AFTER HIS WAR

He was some relation
maybe the husband of some relation
to my grandmother
Bent and slow and thin
emaciated
his hands bony
roped with veins
blue under thin skin mottled with age
After his war
he came home to his life
gassed in the trenches
and drowning now
his lungs whistling
his thin chest grabbing at rarer air
Mostly he sat
moving very gradually from sofa
to recliner and back
to bed bathroom kitchen table
and back
He clung to life
after his war
grinning
although now we know he grimaced
the ivoried teeth
as evenly spaced as a picket fence
skin a faint yellow from the gas

He lived close to our veterans hospital
the long low brick and wooden sided buildings mounted on piers
Administrative area for future wars
as each man stood forward for medical evaluation
the official stamp rendered on our document
"PASSED'
many of us wishing for an exclamation point following
Wait What Passed?
But then there he sat
clad in issued pajama's and robe
thin-soled slippers
slumped into himself
his wife Inez dutiful and kind
at his bedside
And there
finally
he ended his service.

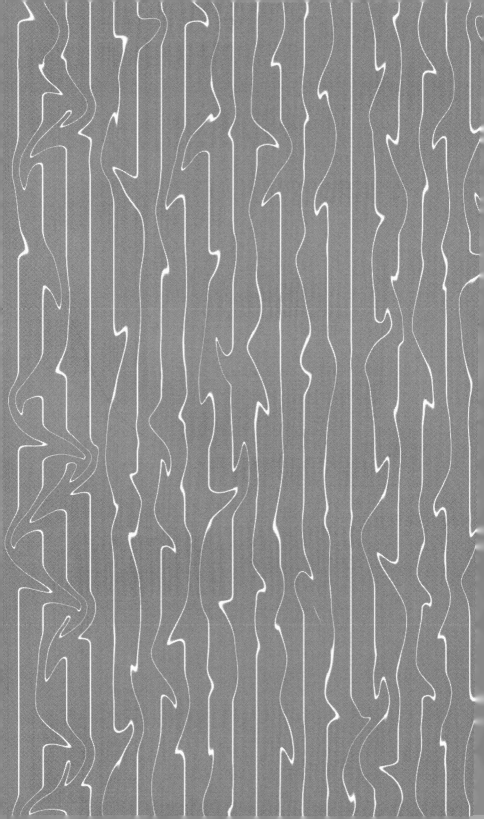

FIELDS OF BONES

Under the sullen paddy waters
where the monster carp feed
relishing weeds, insects, the honey-soil,
cleaning the bones
shining through the dismal waters,
bones left some other time.
(When?)
Who?
The better question.
Next dike over,
a fallow paddy
dried and cracked
like the roof of the mouth of the world
where remnants of armies
lay in dedicated ruin.
And in the distance
huge funeral jars
glistening
like bared bones,
white yellow.
There!
Just behind the jars
a thatched roof,
and people, animals
in a daily routine
for which those bones
fell.

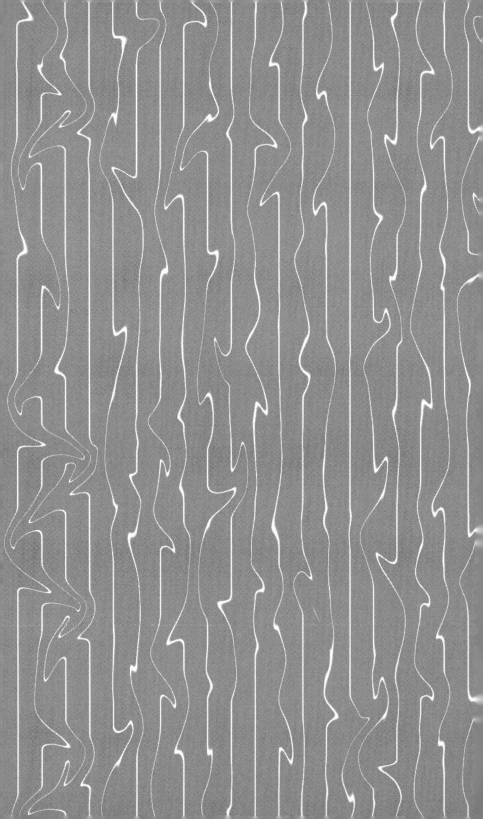

FIRENZE IN JUNE

The four quarters of Firenze ring,
men and music and costumed gladiators,
processions wind through the old City
piazza to piazza.
Tourists jam the cobblestones,
men and women and horses
wander
stone house lined avenues
to the legato cadence of drums.
Stepping forward
teams of men in red, green, white, blue
paw the sanded rectangle
like horses at the gates.
Calcio Storico in Piazza San Croce.
Tickets are scarce.
Best seats
in the windows overlooking the Square.
Blood will fall.
Gladiators will bleed and break.
And through it all,
        her eyes were on the spectacle
        while her heart slowly chilled.
And I,
was left an orphan again.

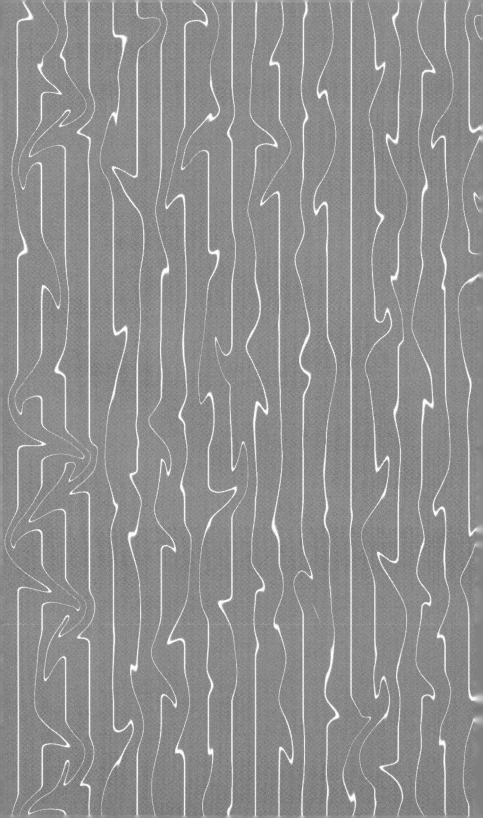

GALENALIA

Romans,
non-voting and voting alike,
giving priase to Minerva,
came with torches this time
while the new priests slept,
and burned the heart of our woods.
At morning
those rough clothed priests,
a new god's mendicants,
briefly stood at the edge of the burn,
tsk-tsking,
then hurried to their new god's temple.
The old gods,
burned out,
swept away,
the granite or sandstone monuments,
headless,
toppled,
crumbled and were no more.
We should have known
for
once were we not
the usurpers?
The new gods and goddesses?
Did we not receive tributes,
sweet wine,
fruits, bread, olives?
But where will we live now?

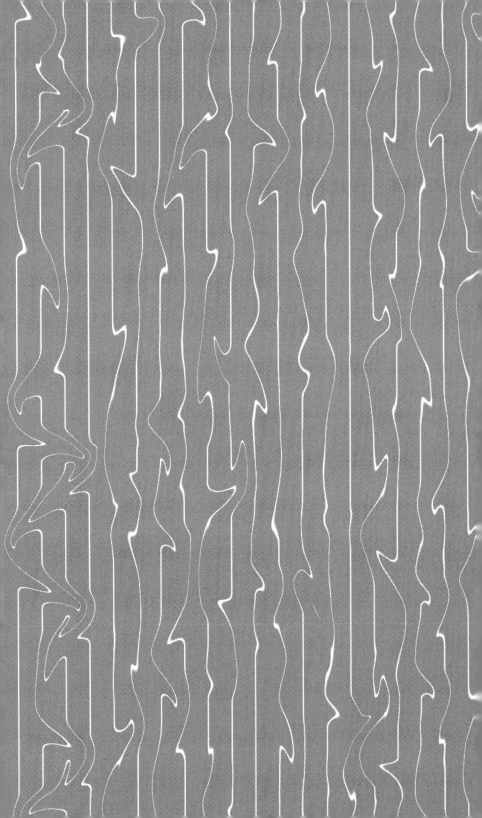

GEOMETRY

Not my favorite school subject,
no, not at all,
            but I never lost interest
or total absorption
in the curve
of a woman's hip.

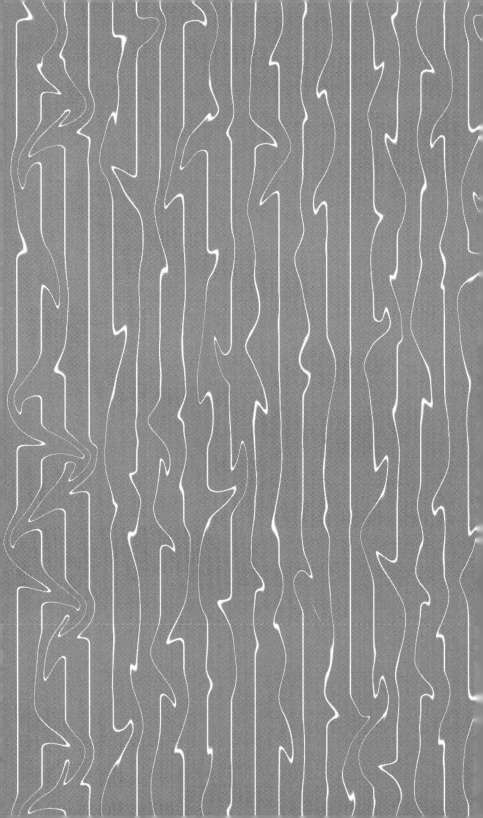

HAIKU

Dark birds on the wires,
      Brittle frost falls like silver.
Who will listen now?

HAIKU #2

Cicadas love songs.
      Our woods echo their passions,
Lingering, then gone.

HAIKU #3

Owl calls at midnight.
      Where were you, from the dark bed?
Some things never die.

HAIKU NO. 4

Lone snake wakes and coils,
      suddenly it is not wet.
We step higher, then leap.

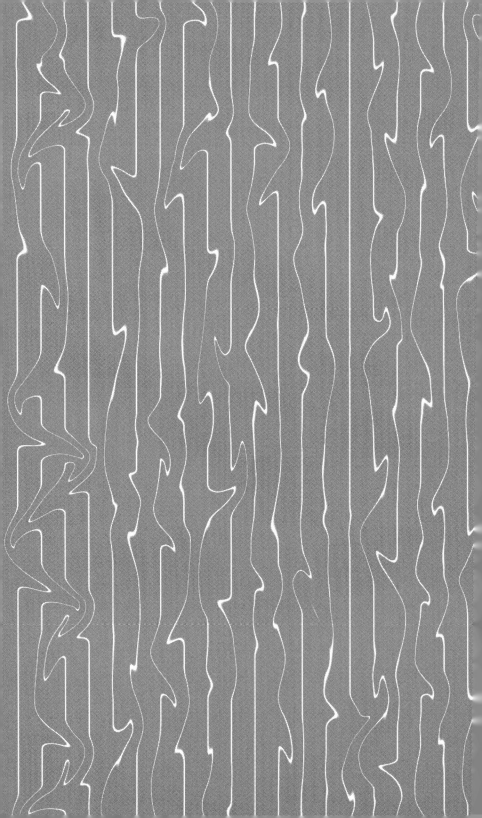

HOW HE DIED

I learned to listen
Sitting in the living room;
Listen to each and every breath caught in his throat.
The breathing caught me,
found me hiding inside my skin.
I would go to his bedroom,
Lean over him,
Hoping that breath would be his last.
The solid oak of a man
Who spread over me
From as far back as I could remember,
Who was often disappointed in me,
unhappy with me,
His eyebrows crawling caterpillar-like
Toward each other.
Now reduced to a frail, old shell,
His breath catching,
clicking in the back of his throat.

As a child,
I learned to soar away from his wrath,
imagined wrath,
Catch the wind and sail far away.
I could become a pirate, a desert warrior, a swordsman,
But I had become his nurse, a sitter.
He had no company to give in return,
The eating of his brain rendering him empty.
But
There, the faint click of breath,
Fainter then
Back in his throat
As he reached for rare air,
As he drowned in the attempt.

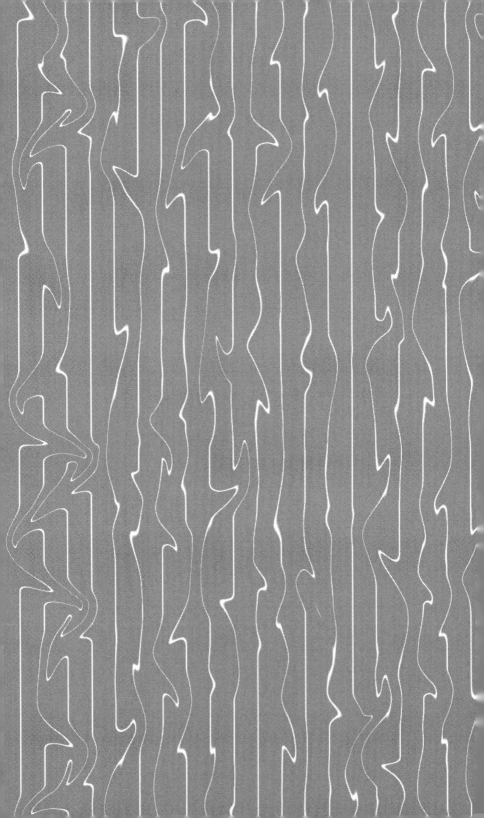

IF I COULD PAINT

If I could paint,
I would never tire,
never find perfection,
never cease the search
for the explanation
into the mystery of a woman's naked back,
her arms cloaked by luxurious sheets
in the early morning summer lightness.
She,
in the open window framed by her hair,
and the eternal pose
of desire.

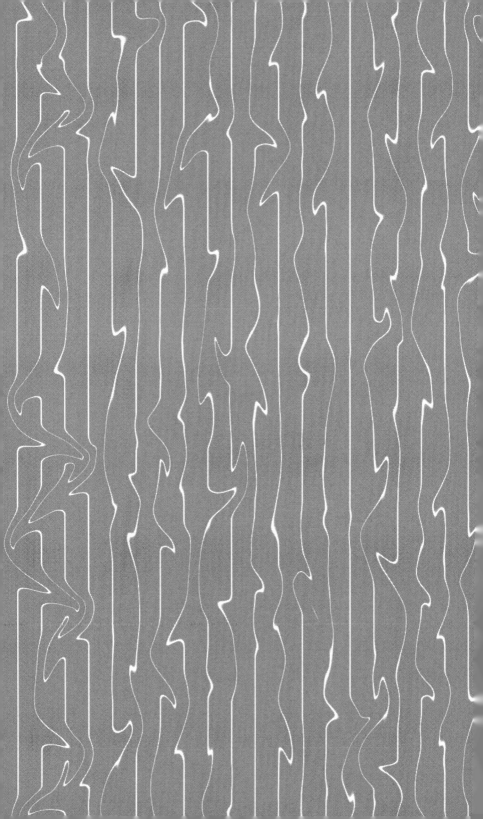

SON

A kite hangs in a Lombardy Poplar tree.
It has spun
Spider-like,
A lacy web through the trees top,
Spun circles in raw Spring winds,
And it smiles forever.
My son speaks of the kite
In wet child kisses.

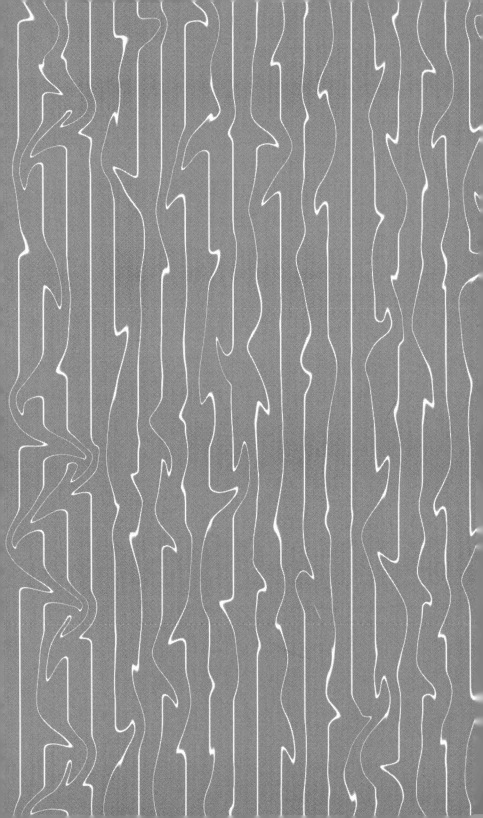

LATE

She wore a school tartan skirt and a white shirt.
The pink backpack
with the Kitty Cat graphic
matched
her pink socks and set off her white tennis.
The braids in her hair,
Tipped with while and pink beads, alternating,
swayed as she bounced along.
Oh to be 8 again!
Her mom held the daughters right hand
in her left,
her right hand kept a small red umbrella over them,
protection from 8:30 AM sun
already hot in late August.
And they were late for school,
both hurrying along the cracked sidewalk,
hurrying towards whatever would be there
for her
this day and everyday.
She looked up at her mom
now and then,
glances,
a smile on her brown face,
going to school,
dressed nicely
with her mom so close.
The hot morning
suddenly full of promise.
We step higher, then leap.

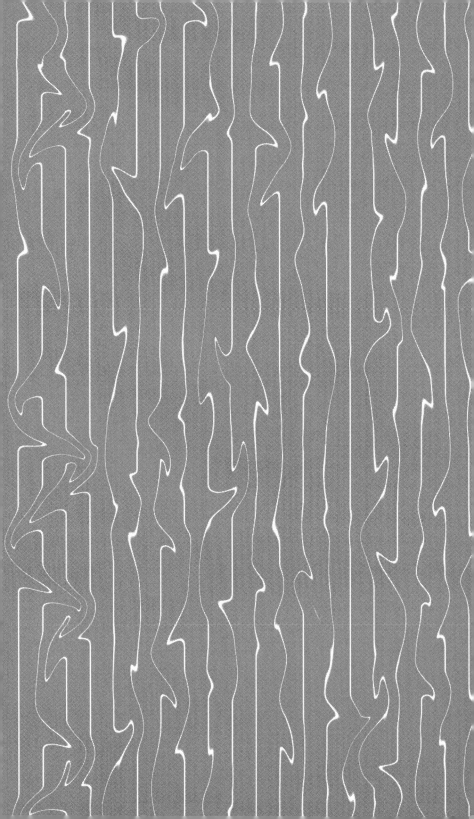

LOS INDIOS DE PENITENTES

Pilgrims, winding through the wearied striations,
stone loose and crumbling,
the paths,
carved by centuries of unhurried feet
unburdened by the miles,
send weathered sandstone and shale
clattering upon the heads of those following.
No one dodges
and the missiles miraculously
strike no one.
The Penitentes
march through the wildernesses,
across deserts,
alkali flats
where only the small untroubled toads,
horned and ridged live,
Satanic in form,
and the little wolves
move silently in the nights quiet dark.
This is Paradise
for those pilgrims given to the Word.

And behind them in the haze of vastness,
spires cast shadows in the sky,
each one named and revered by older religions.
They have torn their flesh,
these Pilgrims,
frenzied in abandonment to their mythical god,
flayed themselves on his altar,
this desert,
they wander.
And on they march
as regimentally formatted
as the ragtag god they seek to please.

LOST

I'm beginning to lose things.
Around the house
        in my closet, kitchen,
and it is a small house;
that flashlight I kept handy to investigate
        weird sounds in the night,
my left cold weather boot,
        a book partially read,
        a recipe for meatloaf.
I search inside, outside, in the car.
I look intensely.
I remember "The Borrowers,"
        and I wonder......?
Yet
there,
In my old photographs from real cameras,
some yellowing,
some in black and white,
        fading
are reminders of great events,
moments of shattering personal history.
Personal.
        And I have also begun
the process of divestiture.
Perhaps things are not lost,
        just misplaced, divested.
Odd coats, shoes, trousers, shirts,
hopefully now worn by men
        or women

in greater need than I.
Even books,
my most sacred of possessions
are being reduced in numbers,
                given away
                 or
                resold.
Anyone for a volume of Descartes?
Im sweeping out the old cobwebs,
replacing them with new strands
that,
I hope,
will last long enough to become old cobwebs.
Or perhaps I will last long enough for that.
                Then!
                There!
Somehow or other,
that left cold weather bottle emerges,
hidden under luggage
ready to travel.
                And the flashlight - Ah HA!
Hidden behind the MacBook Air cover
which remains in upright position.
Hopeful fun signs.
Lost?
Momentarily misplaced.

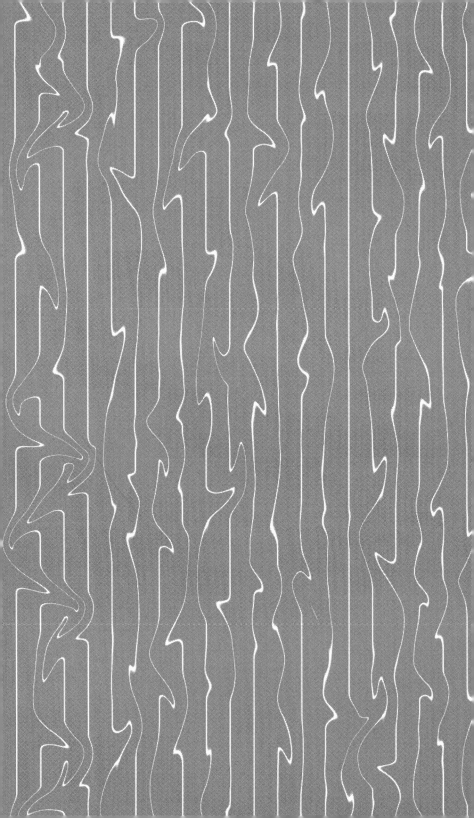

MERRY GO ROUND

She flowered in a desert
brought on by a bad marriage
yet
here she stood
trembling and unsure
but committed with love
or lust
watering her eyes,
filling her heart.

She thought of his job,
how boring
much as he had become.
Which was first?

There he sat,
complacently blind.

And we tumbled
into cars and trucks,
parks and dark secrets,
protesting
what we both knew
to be
what was,
what became.

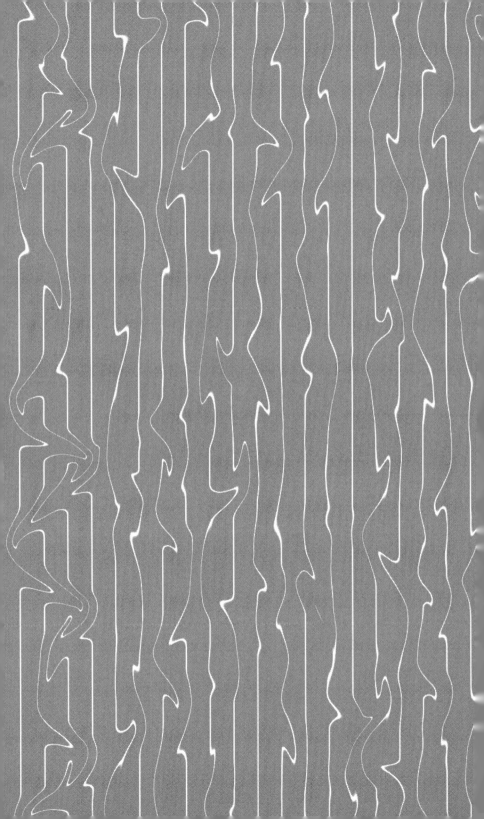

MY COLLECTION

There are two children playing in my garden,
  4th of July streamers tied to their belts;
Innocent and cruel on this hot summer's day;
  I feel the pulse in their throats.

They will sleep tonight on cool, white sheets,
  Locked in private, children's sensuousness;
Waiting the long night in their quiet, white room.
  I can see the flood peak in their dreams.

If I squint against the sun and watch through slitted eyes,
  They are many colors, bouncing in my garden,
Some new specie of royal butterfly;
  I hear the wind from their wings.

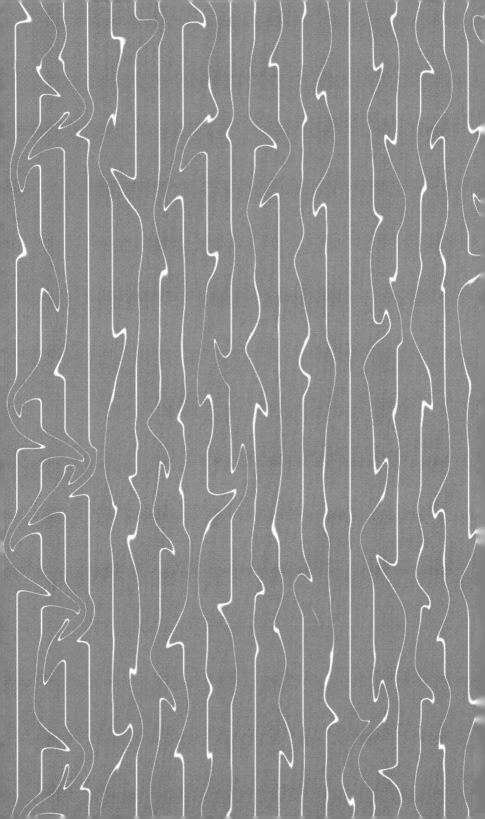

MY HEART

My
            heart is a metronome beatingeverfaster
then   like a composition byCharlesLloyd
Skips when

you   dontexpectit.   No
                there
then up again
      and in its cruel rhythm
the welling of the blood through myveins veins veins veins
      only to   wait againandagain

        At one time
I waited in one early night
some years ago
                                    for it to
                give

me

                            one more
pump   and it
                        Did. Finally

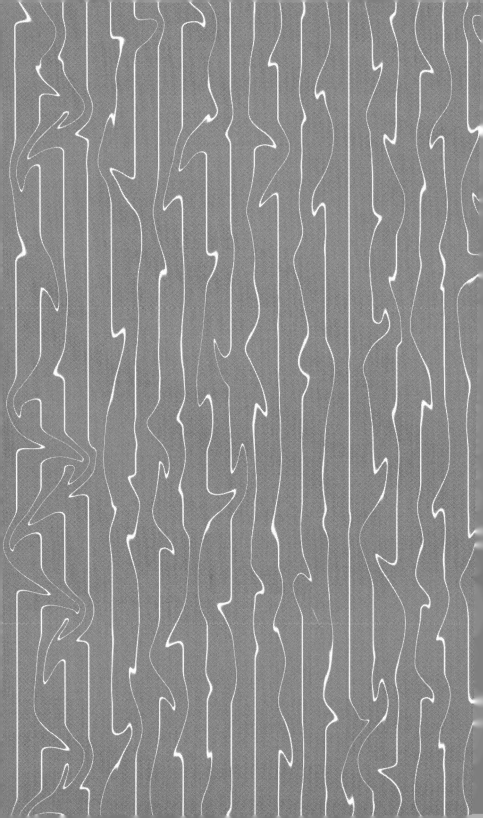

HISTORY

I wish I knew my history.
Maybe ancestry, too.
My mother's side
          written
          while my father's side
eludes me,
Drifts like smoke in cold winter winds.
Some know both sides,
mother and father.
And recite them
in earnestness and intensity.
While I dream and fantasize
          of romantic, quixotic familia.
While my mother's barber father,
heart-diseased and fragile,
lived and raised prized chickens,
Winners of international awards and international sales.
Chickens.
Old man in Southern white linen.
With his chocolate gift
from Hershey's
descending from the bus.
 He was like Jesus.
Chocolate with his war coupons.
Dead.
History.
Where may I read mine?
Who will write it?
Or evolve it?
Or solve it?
And yours?

ONE FINAL LAST LOOK

That bit of lace
peeking over her black sweater
as delicate and unattainable
as ever.
I would never see it,
fully,
nor the sweet curve of her breasts
under that lace,
no, not me.
Only in my imaginings.
But there in those hazel eyes,
their frank and direct gaze
seared me;
I could feel my heart burning,
and wondered if she could feel it, too.
Intense.
Behind her knowing glances,
an unalterable sadness
in the little crow's feet
at the corner of each eye.
So,
we left each other,
Her last look,
then,

her head turned away,
and an ending.
The walk to her home,
bleak and cold,
and her heart
turned from light that was my sun
to a chill.
Those slow footsteps
with only the faintest hesitation.
Goodbye.
Over her shoulder.
The lace curtains shuddered
as the door slowly closed.

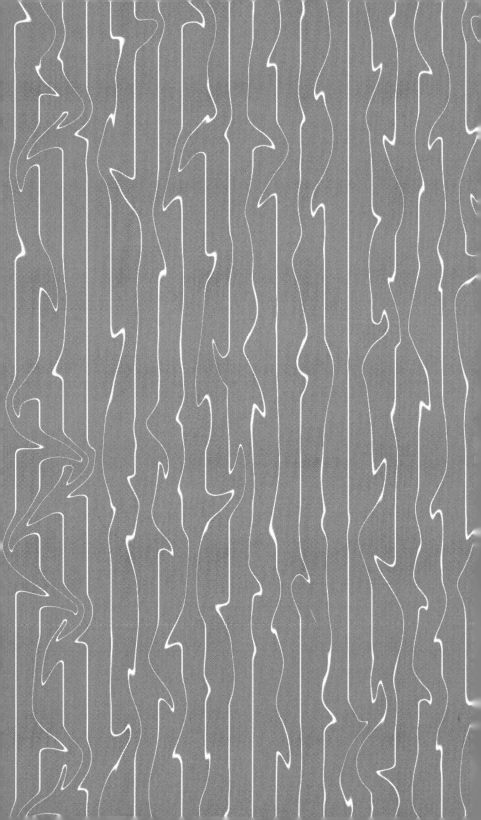

PAPER LANTERNS

We bought them in the bay-side market.
Lit the candle in each base.
We held on to them,
    watched the heat fill them.
They swayed in full illumination
    and
we launched them
over darkling bay waters,
watched them sway and dance
in the water's warm breeze;
watched them,
    sadly,
as they fell flaming;
Fell. Fell. Fell
twisting and hissing
    Into black waters.

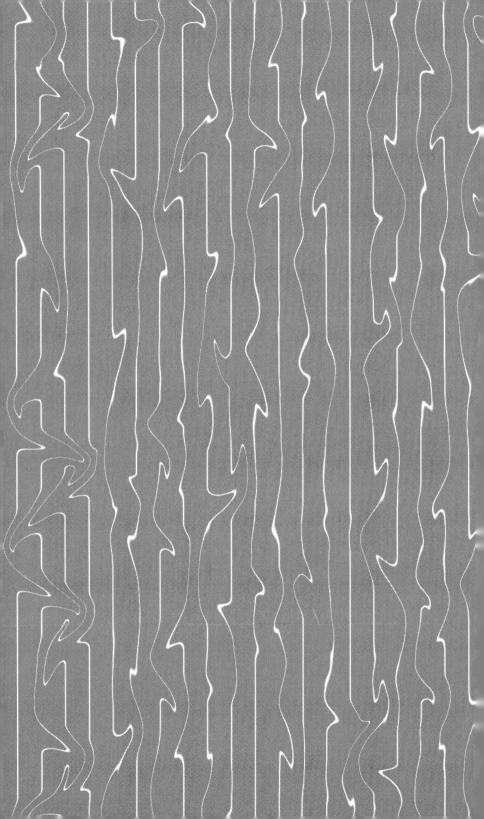

POUND IN A CAGE

Crouched in the steel.
listening intently
to the rhythm of boys sticks
thawhackwhackwhackwhack
along the bars,
his head bent under his shoulders,
holding his raft together,
his 6'X6' cage
satisfying to his American tormentors,
pleasing his Italian detractors.
Pound grew ragged,
the Cantos unspooling in his head,
he hobbled into numerous hearings,
his testimony as ragged as his beard,
unrepentant and unpleasant,
Finally,
sent on to Washington,
to "rest" and recover,
deny his fascist leanings.
The Cantos fresh,
unrivaled, unparalleled.
He preferred small spaces,
his closet, a pantry, under the bed,
contained and expansive,
as his poetry soared.
Pound in society,
the Cantos on paper,
he rested and lectured,
leaving those petals of poetic blossoms
preserved in countless texts,
on shelves in poets brains,
the culmination of his caging in Venezia!

REFLECTIONS AT 18 MILES

No one met me that drear morning.
No one in the parking area.
Cold wind from the northwest,
always in your face.
The hills,
short, steep, bitter,
and unrelenting,
punished me for whatever sins
I had committed,
or
ever thought I would commit.
Where was my life bound?
Over the next cruel hill?
At the end of this run,
or
the next?
How had I reached this single,
ferocious place in my life?
What brought me to it?
Was I happy?
Would I ever be happy?
What was happiness?
Another mile passed.
Fifteen down and down and down
hills
not yet encountered
I would go.
Now a car passes,
heads craning to peer at this fool.
Another barrels towards me,

I step aside,
leering at the driver
who pays me no mind
so intent is he on his common destination.
The next and last mile,
here now,
is downhill,
much as my life at that moment,
And much as I endure that,
it offers respite
from the ceaseless up hill battles.
More traffic now,
and I am just a thing moving,
a frost streaked,
hoary runner
covered in colorful attire,
with an icicle dancing under his nose.
And then I am at 18 miles,
unrepentant now,
laughingly pugnacious
at my momentary victory.
But
in two days
I will be here again,
for twenty.

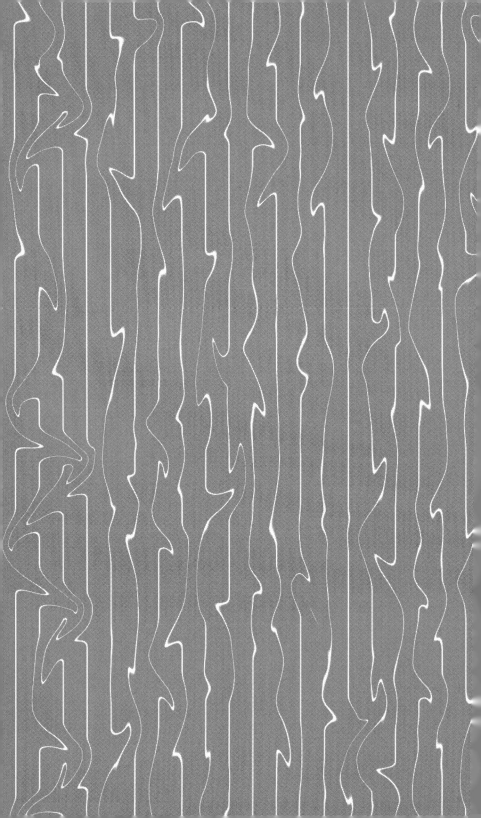

REMINDERS

I was today reminded
(by a younger woman's glance
her eyes lingering momentarily
then flicked on)
that I am
at an age
where I live between two worlds.
I seem younger
but I am not.
My credit is shaky
yet I pay my bills.
My eyes are blue as ever
but I see poorly.
I am still fit (overweight a bit)
but it seems wasted.
I own little. Really.
I am part of many. Really.
Sons I've spoken of before,
written to and of,
loved long time.
My coat is woolen,
but my heart strides on. Haltingly.
My car needs work.
My shell is cracked.
My legs want to be stressed,
lungs covet a gasp
while knees remind me
glory is indeed
fleeting.

SPILLED BEER AND WET PAPERS

On my bar stool,
I am the one-eyed King
in the land of the Blind.
On my bar stool
I can see for miles and miles and miles and miles and
MILES!
On my bar stool
I am Peter Sellers,
Samuel Clemens.
My talents perpetually fill my raised glass,
and I hear sonnets
whispered in my ears,
challenging me,
entreating me,
yes,
even threatening me.
Still,
here I sit
surveying all
with equal insouciance
and disguised fury.
I toast our barkeep,
dribbling beer onto my shirt,

dripping from my chin
which I wipe
more or less,
surreptitiously.
My right hand snags the beer glass
on the return acknowledgement,
pooling beer onto the stained, worn wooden bar,
and my precious poems,
my inked papers' hieroglyphics,
merging into a language
only I can translate.

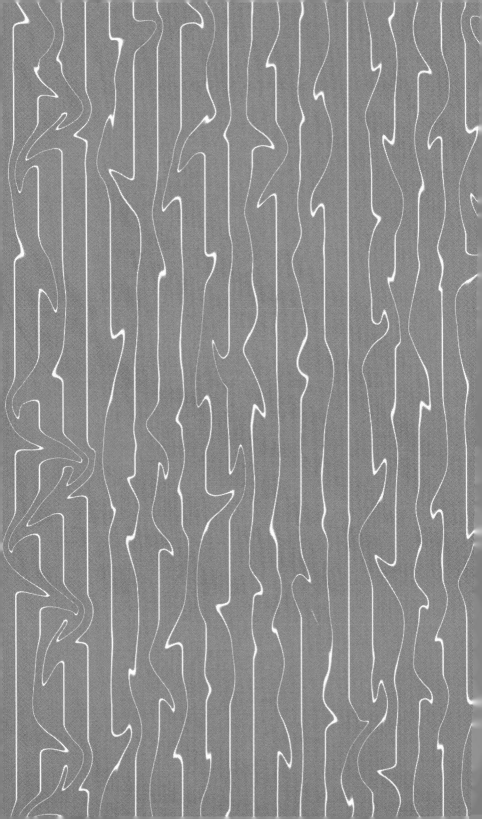

SUN DOGS

Was a lovely afternoon
        aboard my sloop
Her red bikini an invitation,
        a warning?
While I as captain, crew, mate
from our port tack
        spy a parhelion,
my sun dogs,
twinning to port and starboard
the clouding days leashed pets..
I was briefly led to Odysseus,
his sails full,
purple,
searching Mare Nostrum
for a swifter return to Telemachus and Penelope,
        her weaving half finished.
I hear him cry out,
"Draw your bow, draw your bow!"
        While I drowse in the stern
        from wine and lust,
squinting at my filled sails,
the suddenly straining jib,
hear the hiss of parting seas,
        and a woman in a red bikini.

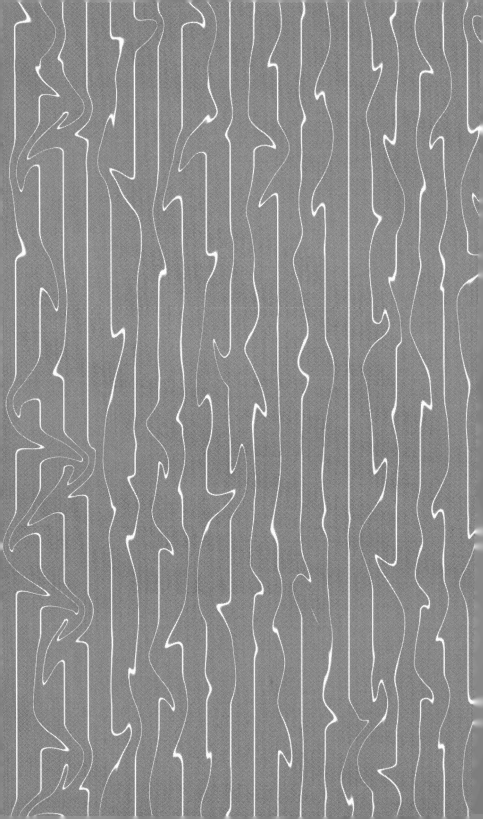

THE RIVERS COURSE

Love is a river
running from the heart to the soul
in full flood.

It roils and rushes
tumbling all in its wild plundering
sparing nothing and no one.

When it is dammed
against its willful plunging
both heart first
then soul
wither in hunger.

In those who have chosen
not to love fully and without recourse
the emptiness withers all else.

Love is a river
turning from the heart to the soul
in wild abandon.

.

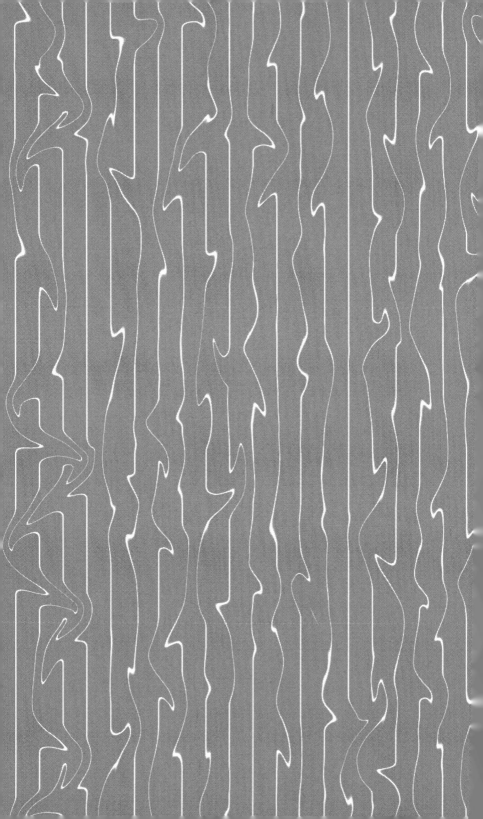

THE WOMEN WALK THE WOLVES

Above the ruins of Athens
Along the red rocky paths,
The women walk the wolves
And the men walk the dogs.
It is as ancient as the cracked boulders
Quarried to build the base of the Acropolis.
Only the women know the truth.
Walking among the twisted and stunted olive trees,
Many more ancient than the ruins,
Walking where the timeless voices
Speak in visions,
The women walk the wolves
And the men walk the dogs.

TROTSKY IN THE DESERT

Shunned in Marmara.
Exiled to various countries.
settled in Mexico,
wife and son saddled with Trotsky's
     high blood pressure,
and
there was Frida,
and of course, Diego.
Where will it end,Trotsky asked?
     But he knew,
of course,
     he knew
where it would end.
Not in Frida's bed,
her breasts, his dreaming,
her heart as cold as the pick
     entering his brain.
He wandered the desert,
alone,
biding his time,
writing, writing.
Watched the small, fast desert hares
     Spring and sprint,
then,
     stop abruptly,
their hearts wildly beating,

waiting the guns retort.
Trotsky waited,
his blood thickening,
    welcomed the assassin's final move.
Thrust out his arms
Shouting,
    "I am dead! Long live the revolution!"
And Natalia wept bitter tears
while Frida mourned his death.
    And then,
Retreated to Diego
and her patrons.
Trotsky,
happiest in the desert.

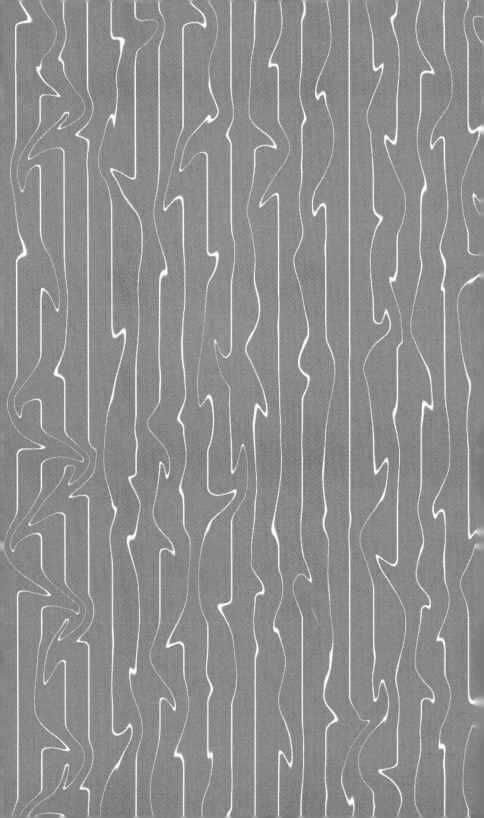

WHAT SHE MEANT

She said.
I don't really know why I am
the way I am
but
I am.
It shining in her eyes
that lingering lost-ness
what I think I've lost in mine.
She said.
Why are you
like you?
and I had to let it go,
look her in her eyes,
that lost-ness
 filling my little boat of declaration,
and I had to say,
how else would I be?

GHOST SEASON

Neatly aligned stones
some few leaning towards one another
in deep conversation overcoming the concrete dividers
Protestant with Catholic
Latvian with Mississippian
Only whites here
dead white people
through the stone orchard
which bears no fruit
but separates colors.

behind the century old cedars
fronting a crude gravel road
winding its circuitous meander from the highway
is the distant edge of the stones
and monuments
faint fog cloaks
cedars, pines, holly trees
clothes them
in their solitary sentinel duty,
shrouds them
as they speak
whispering secrets of the dead
found there.

The names of towns and families
dates of a distant past
are gathered in this one place
fathers and sons
mothers and daughters
grandparents and distant relatives
pass eternity here
whispering their secrets
Only the grave diggers
all black men
with backhoe and shovel
hear the stones,
make no comment
relishing shared death
and the muting of all color.

54194543R00033

Made in the USA
Columbia, SC
27 March 2019